Bird
PARADISE

GRAYSCALE COLORING BOOKS

VOLUME 2.

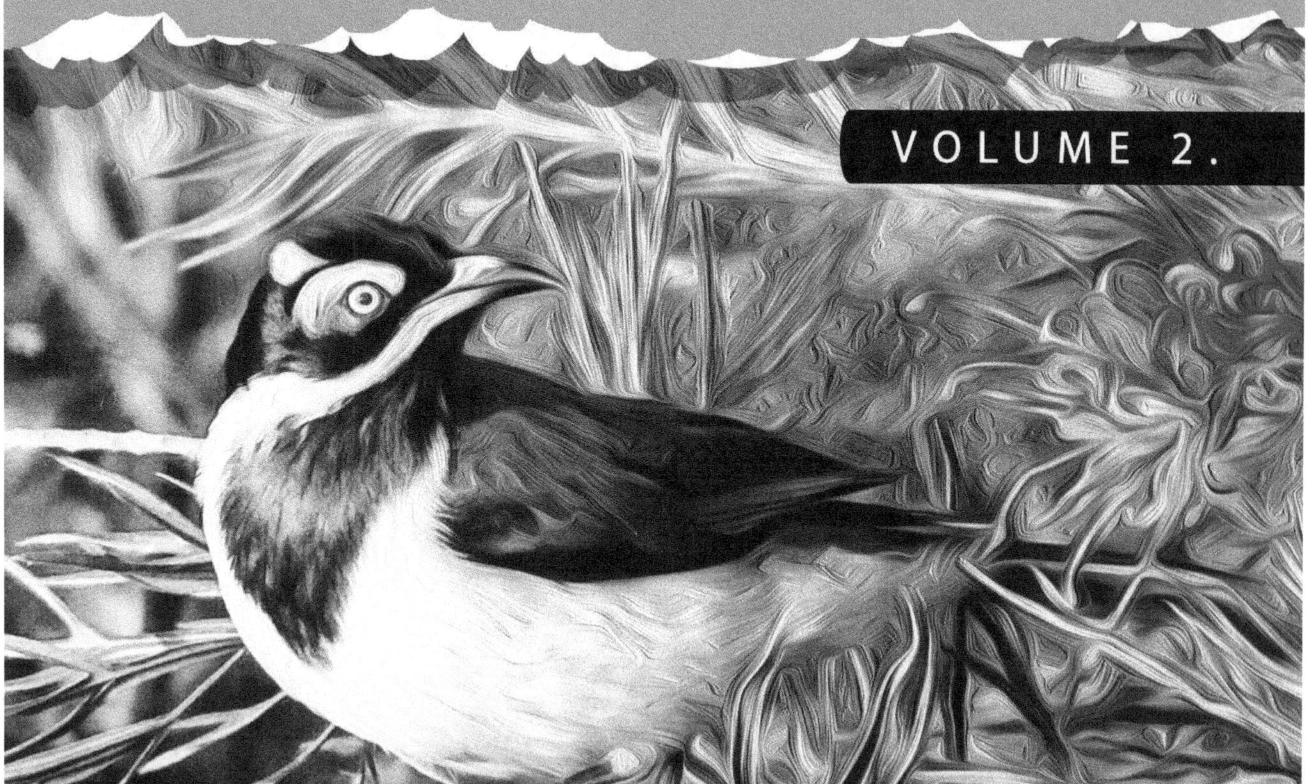

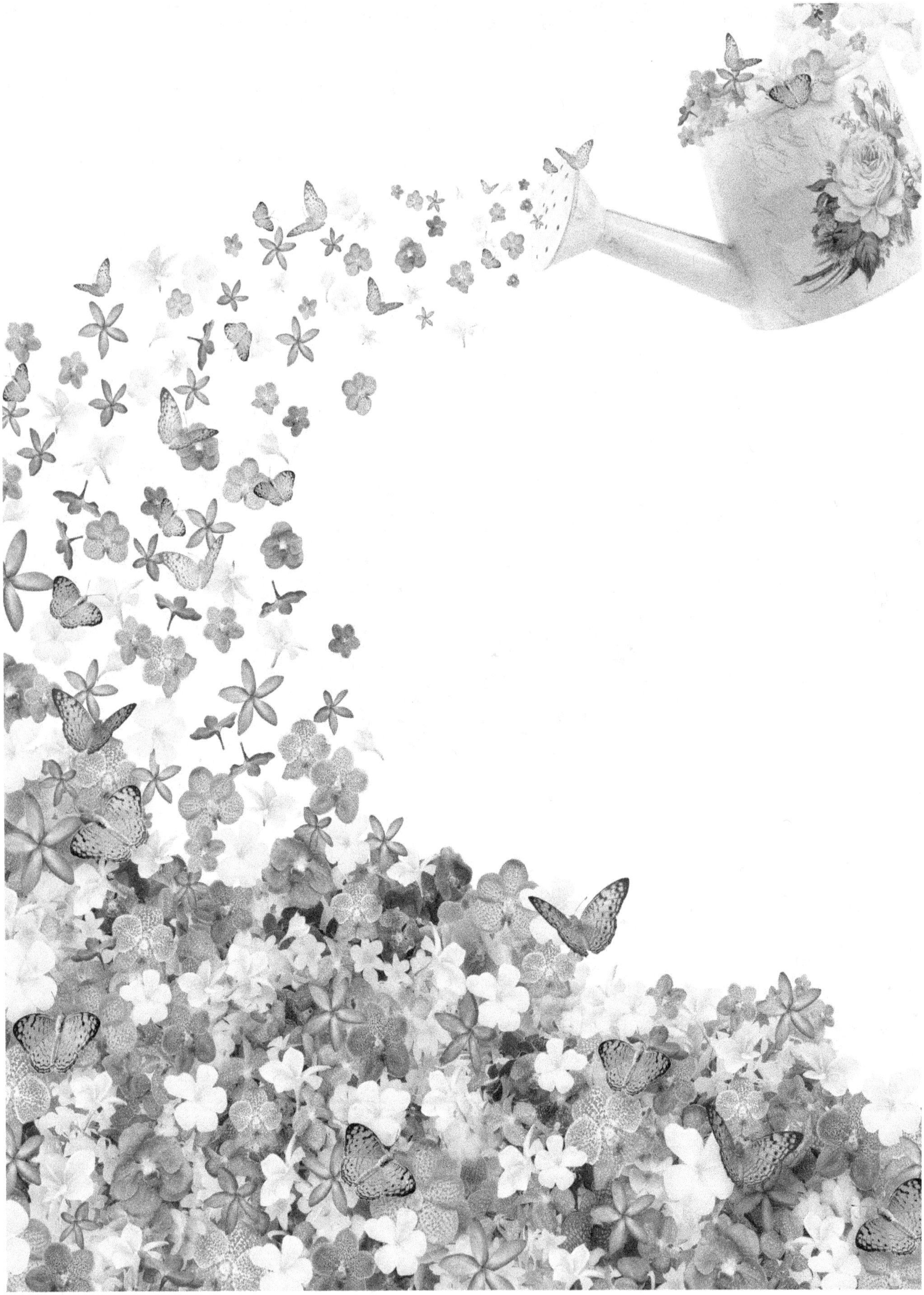

COLOR TEST PAGE

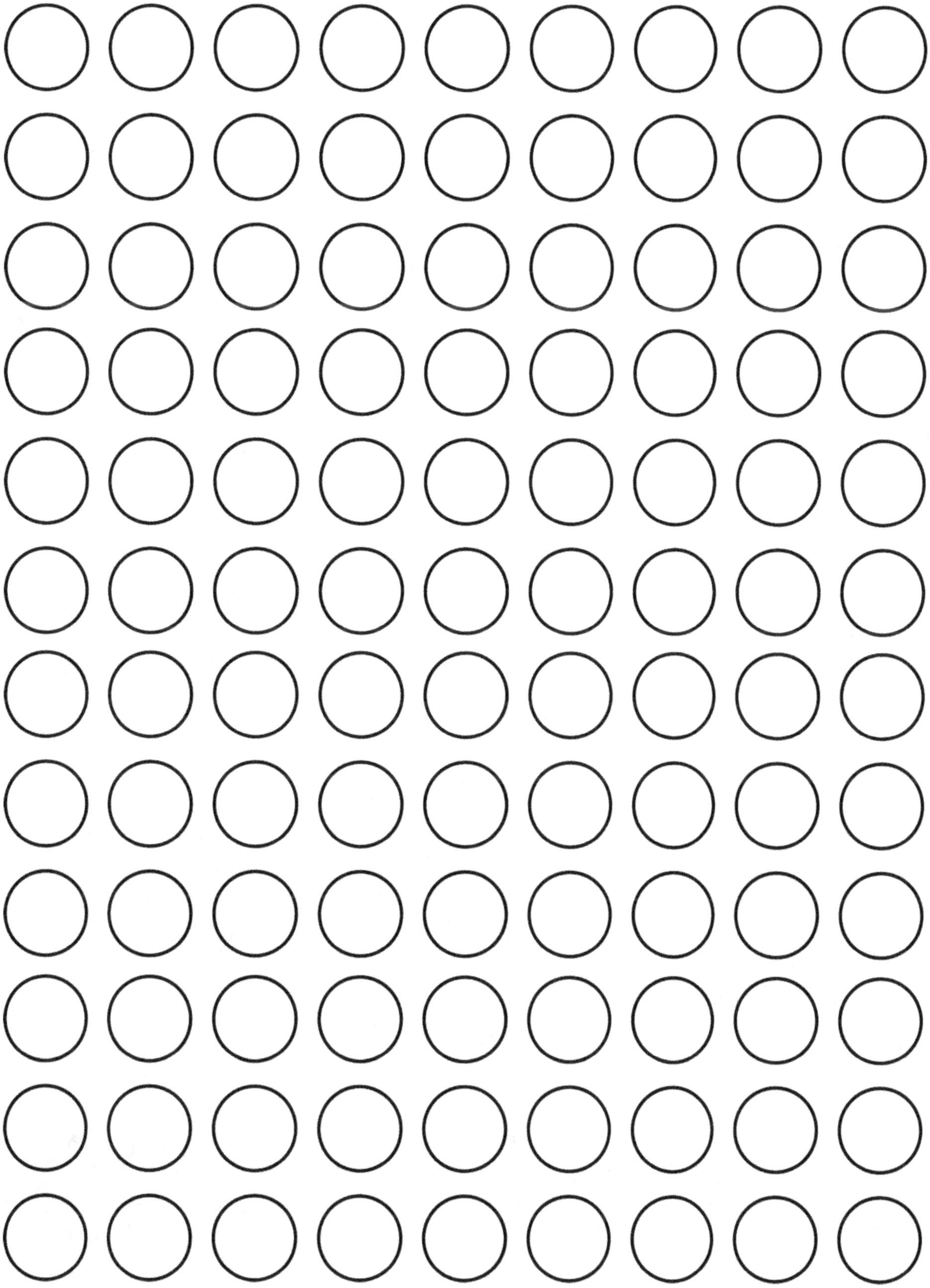

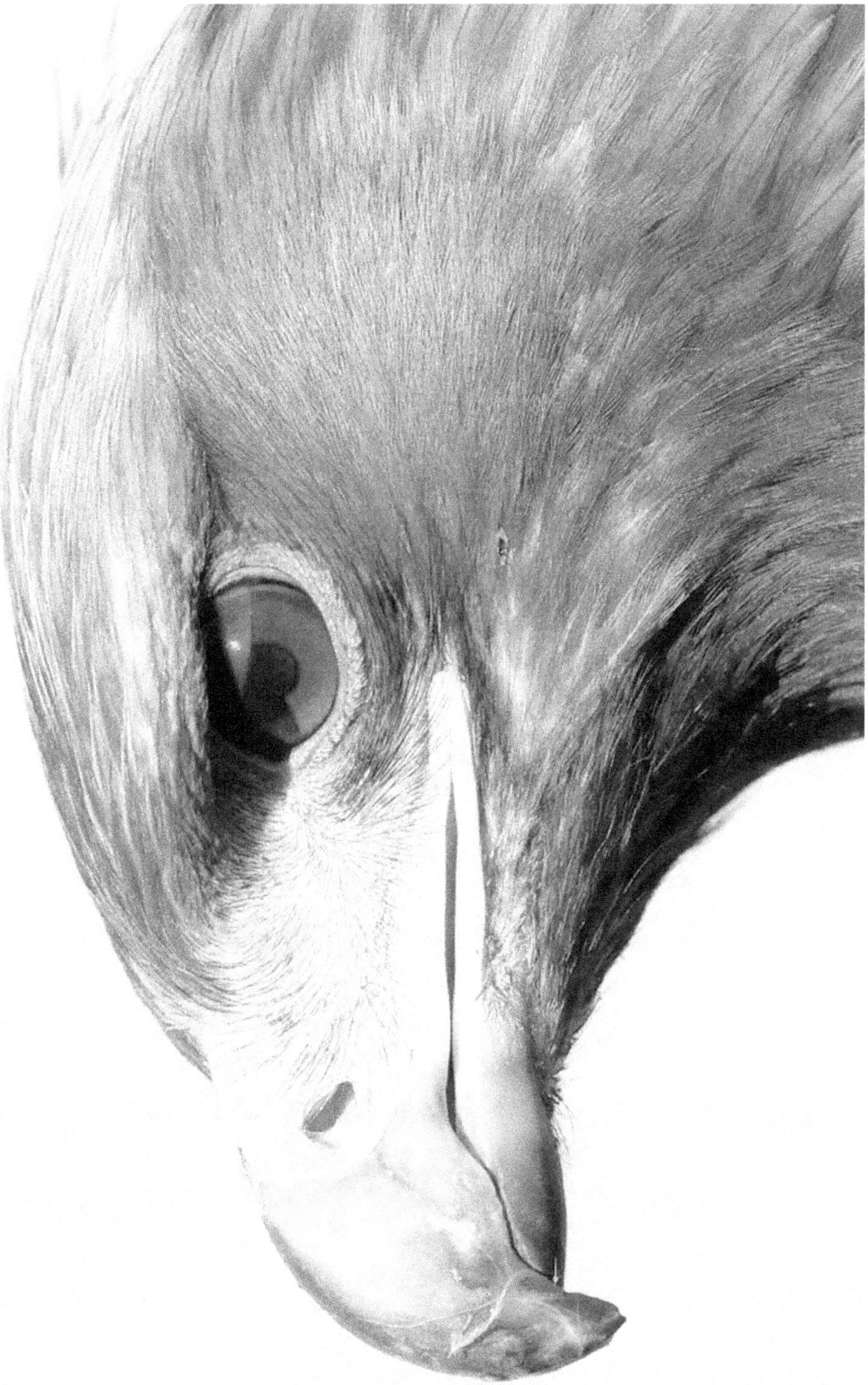

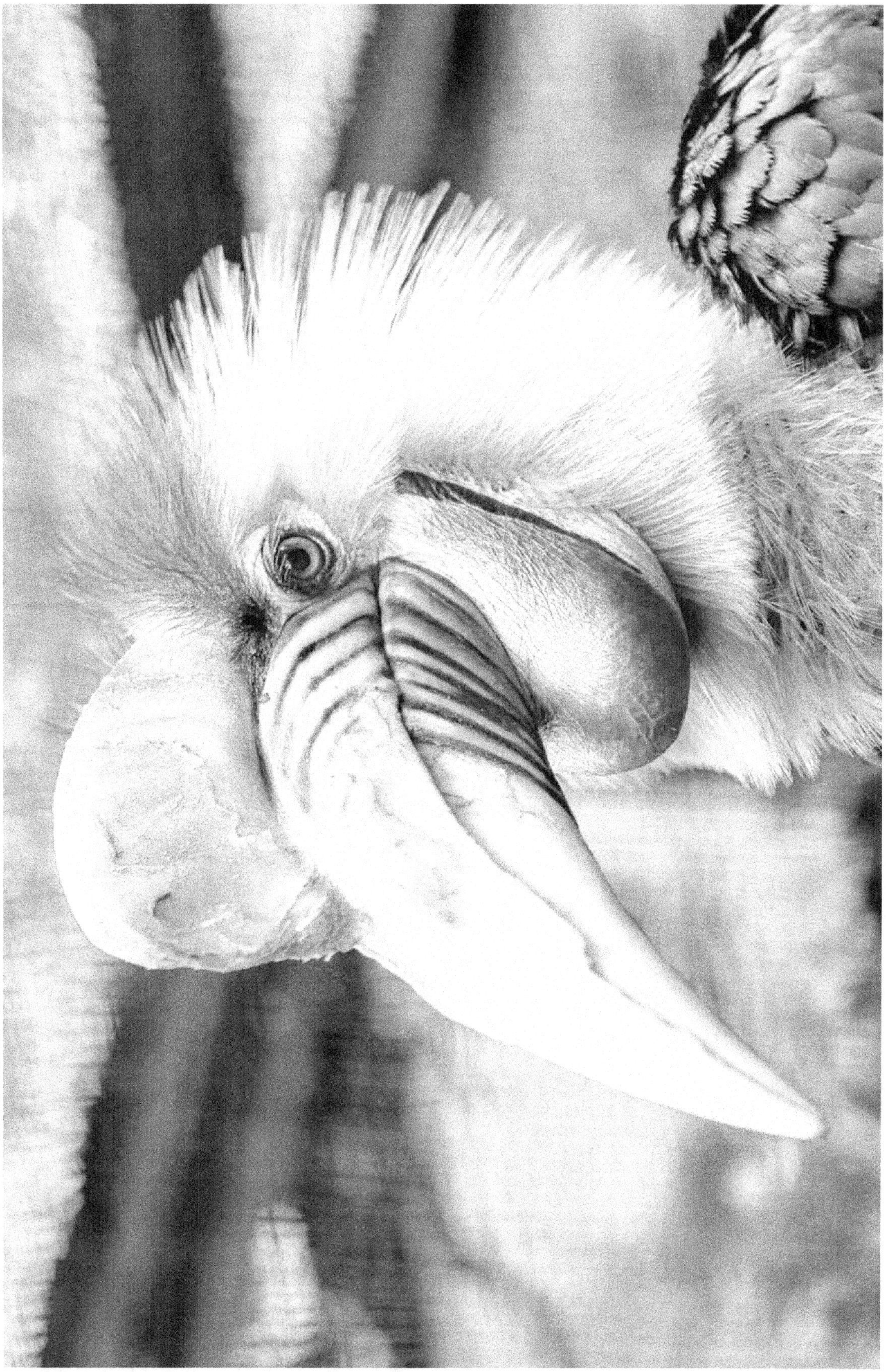

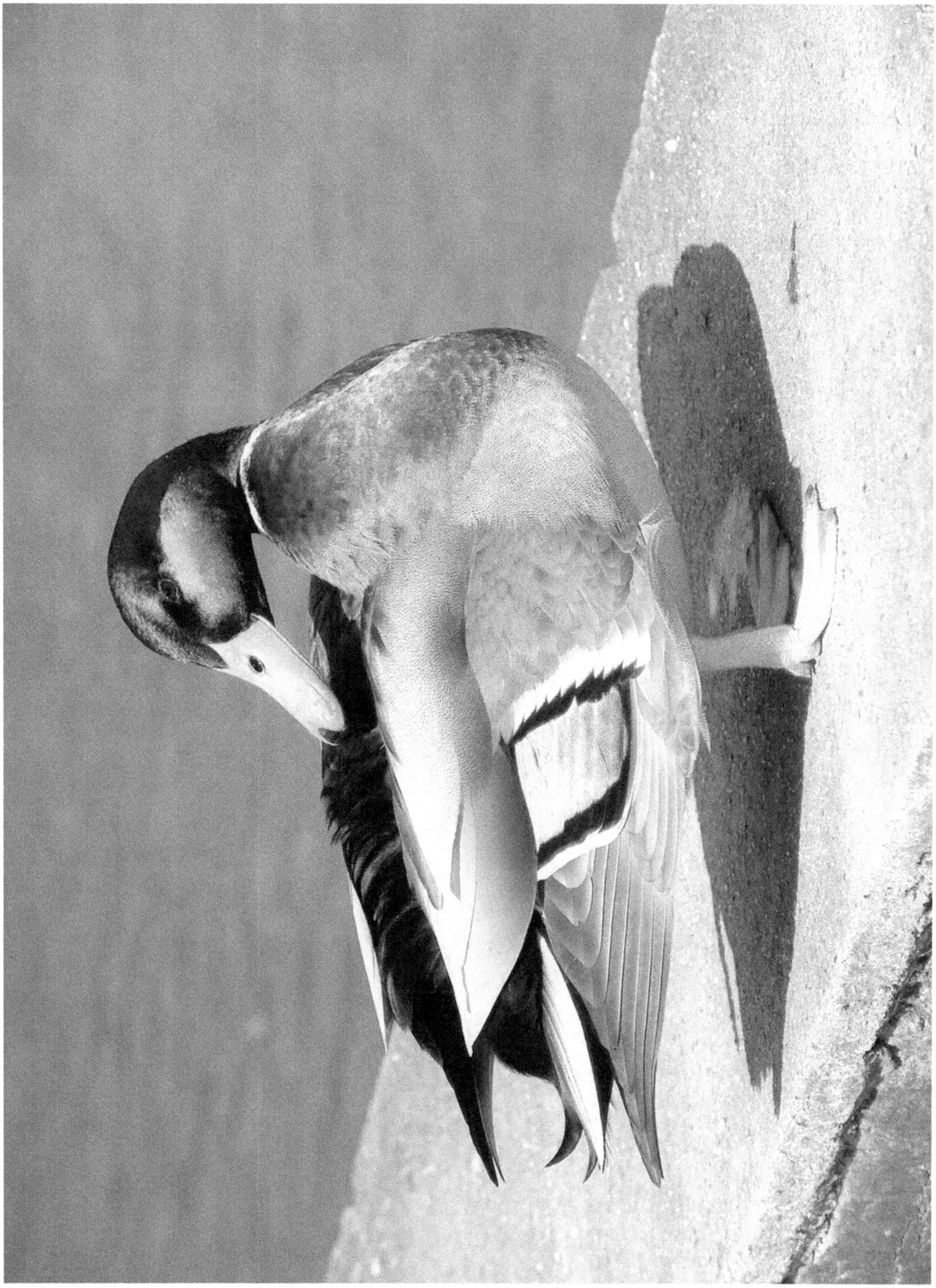

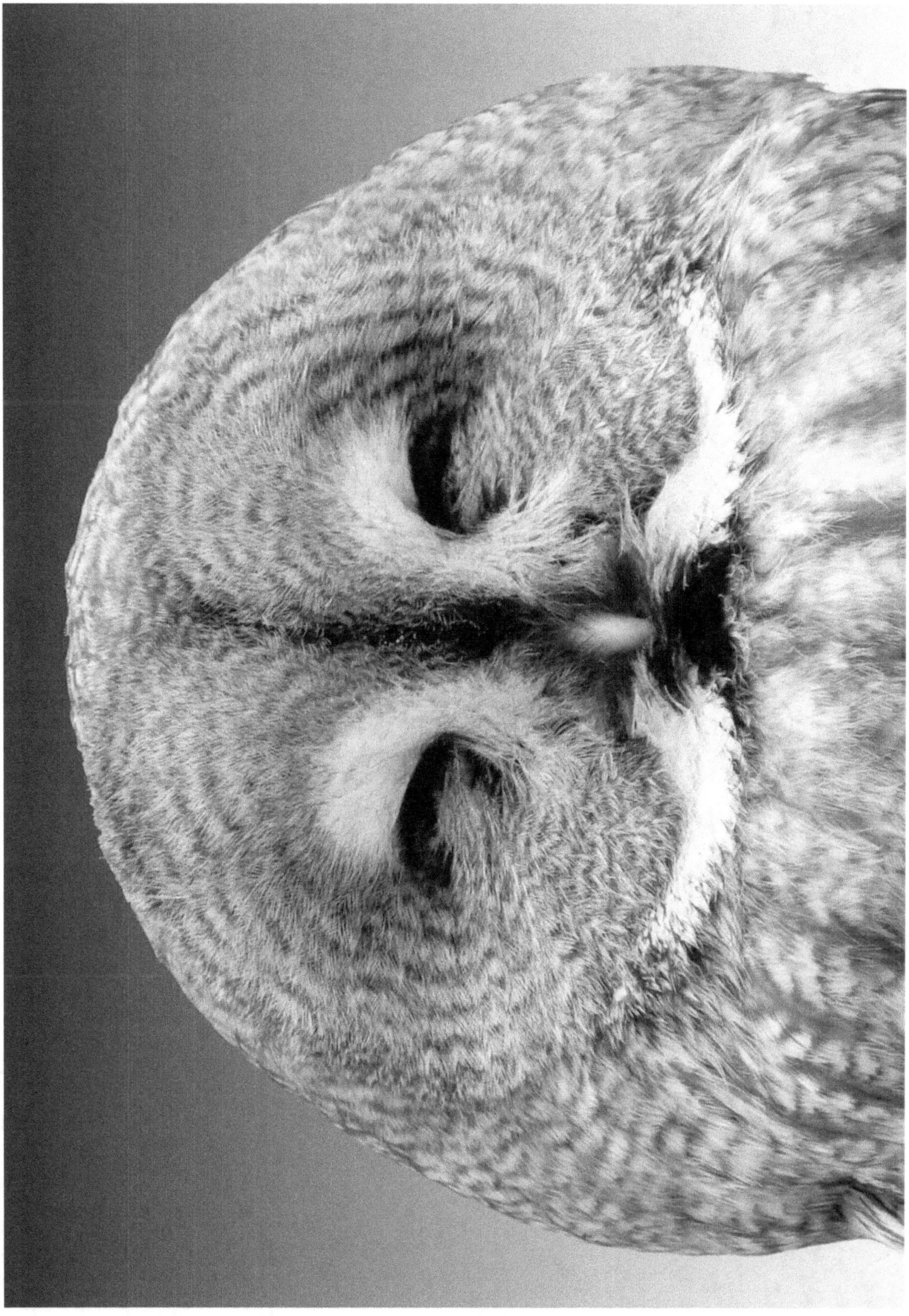

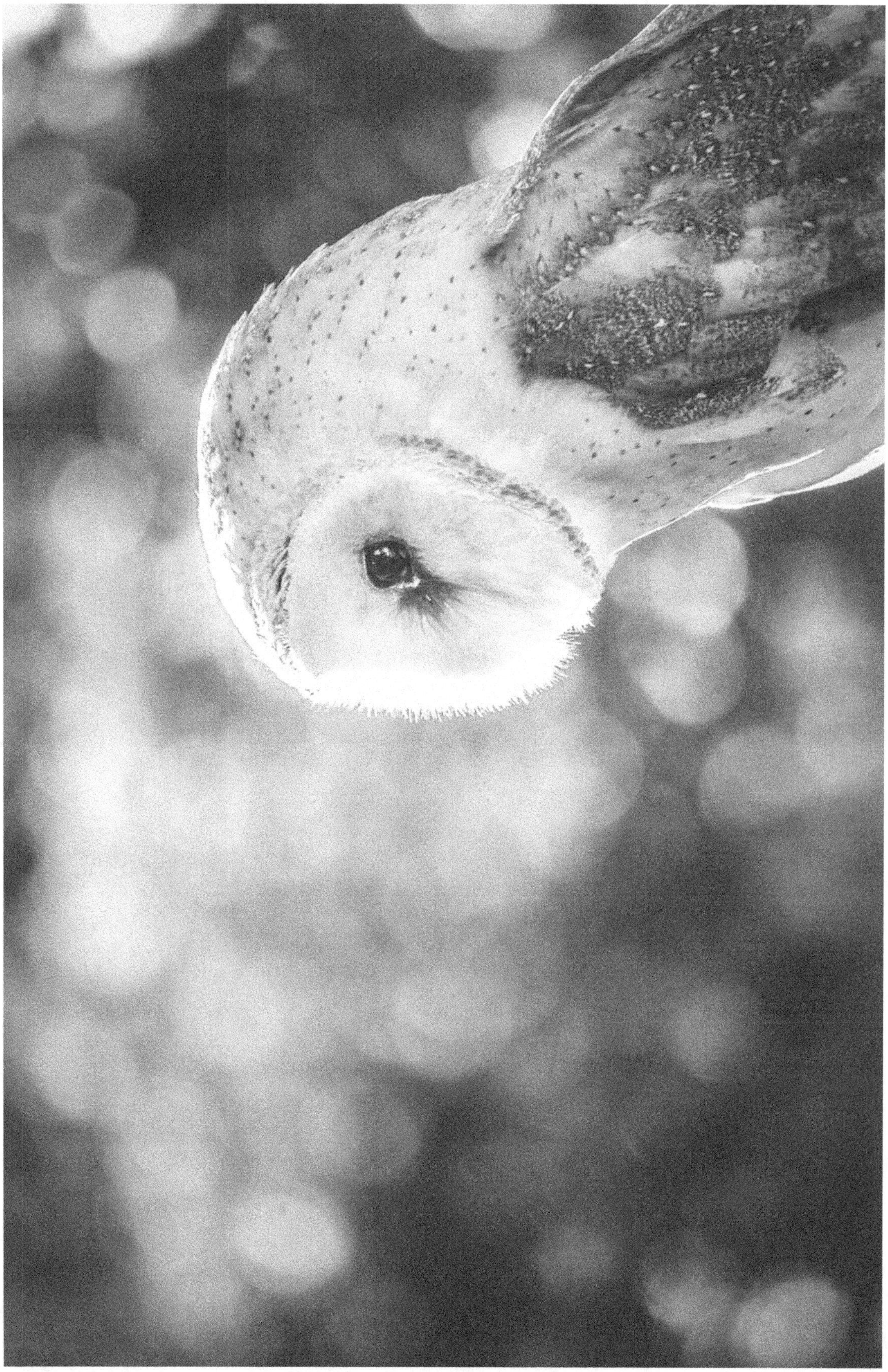

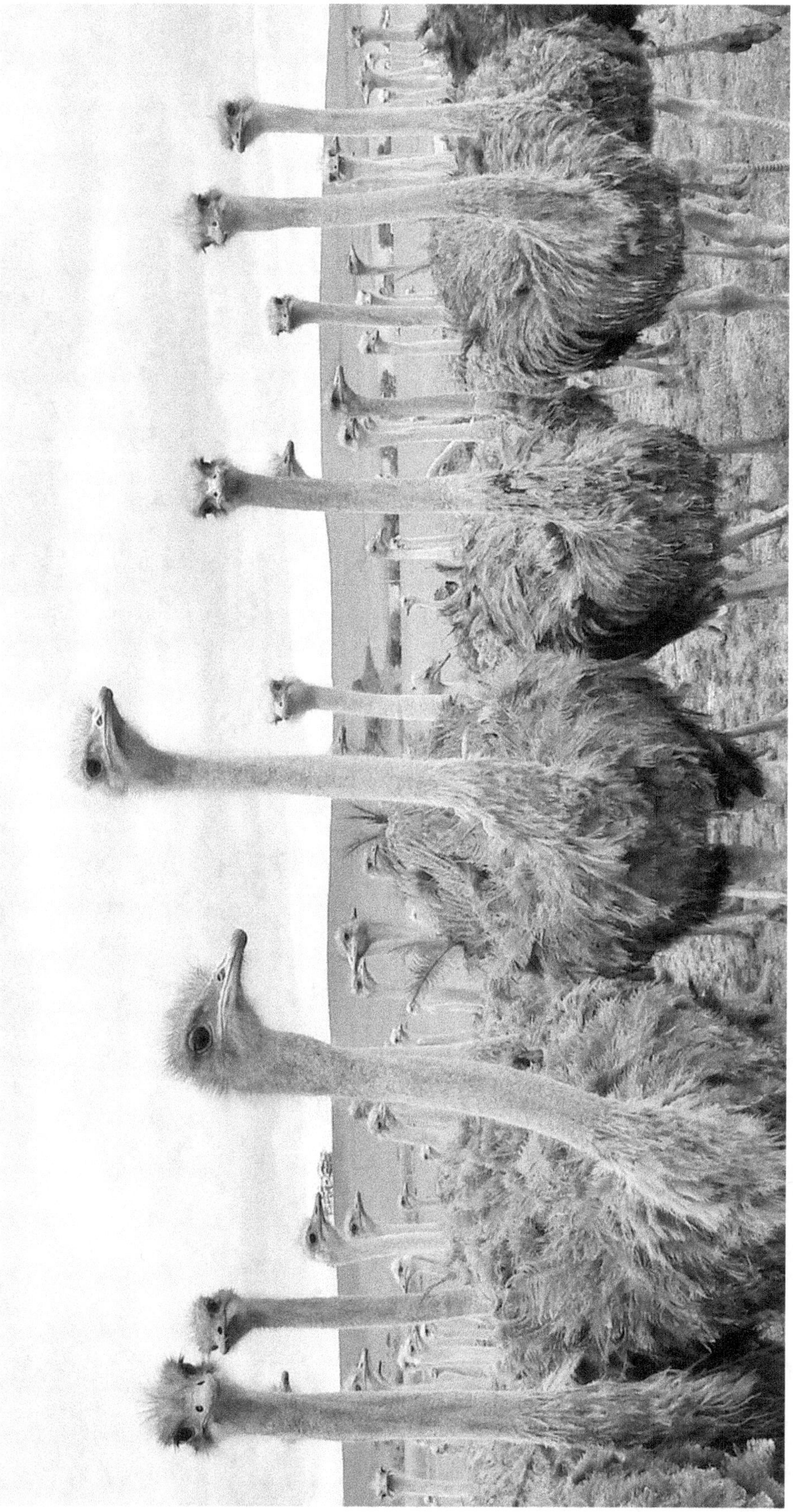

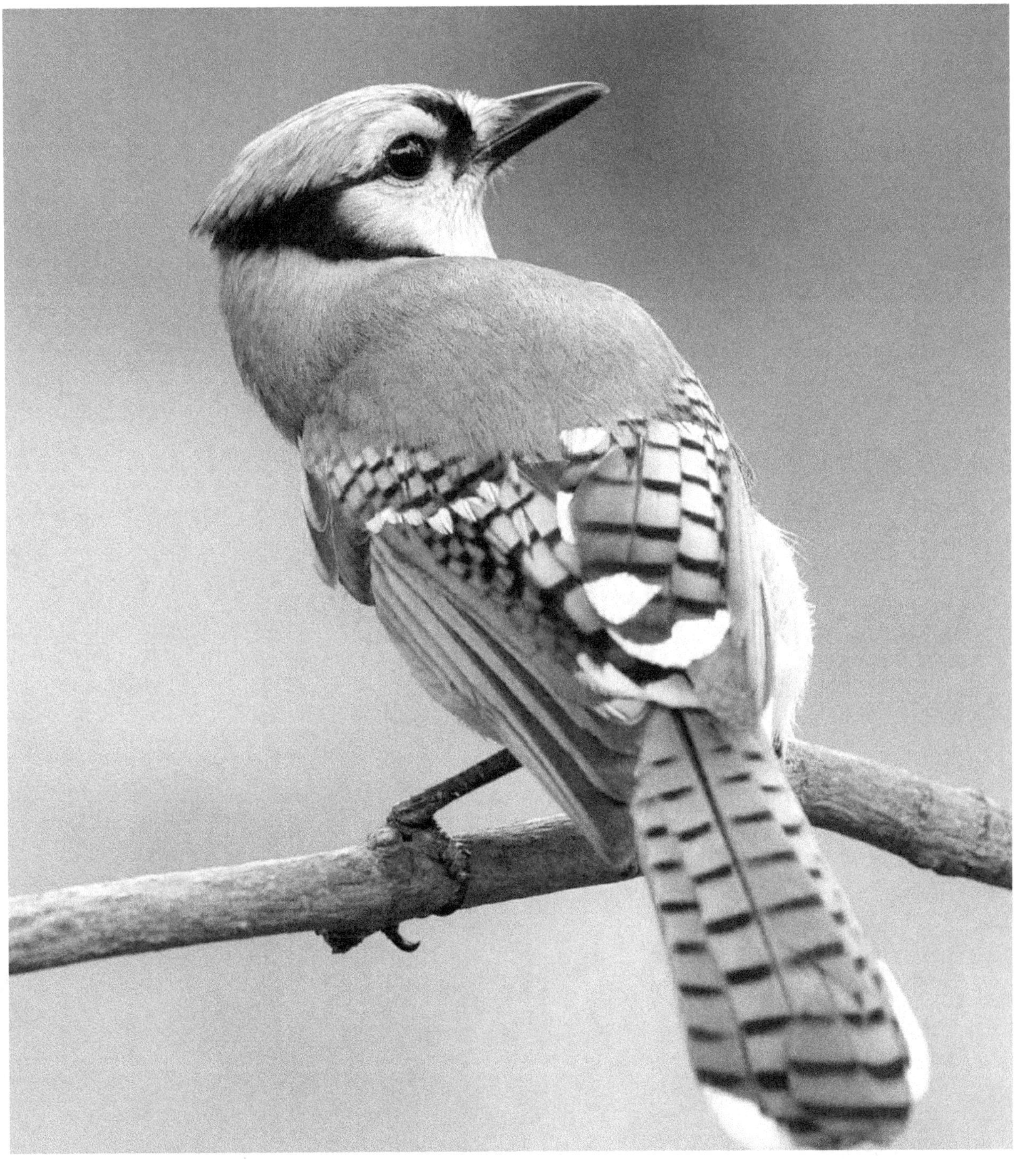

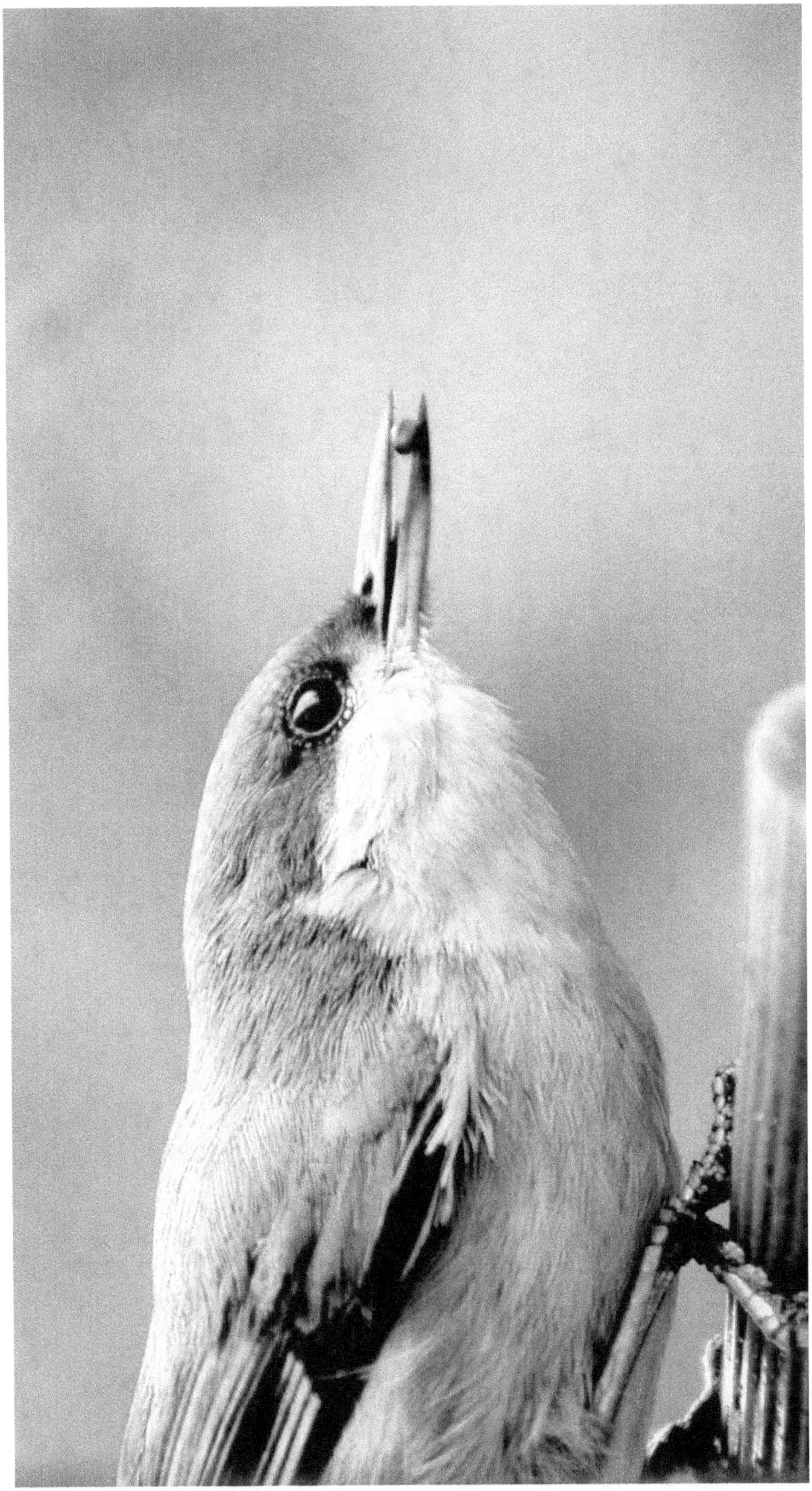

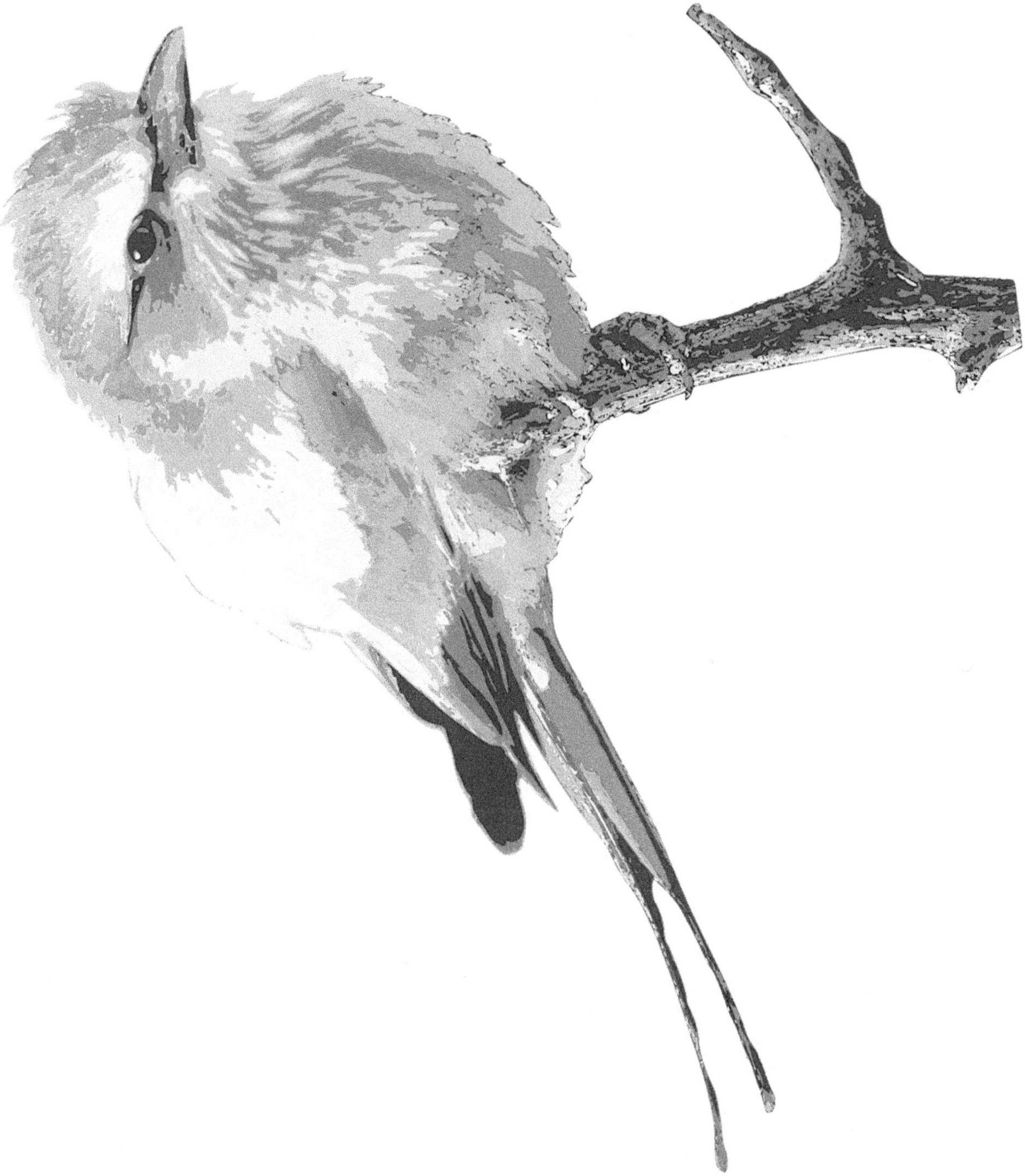

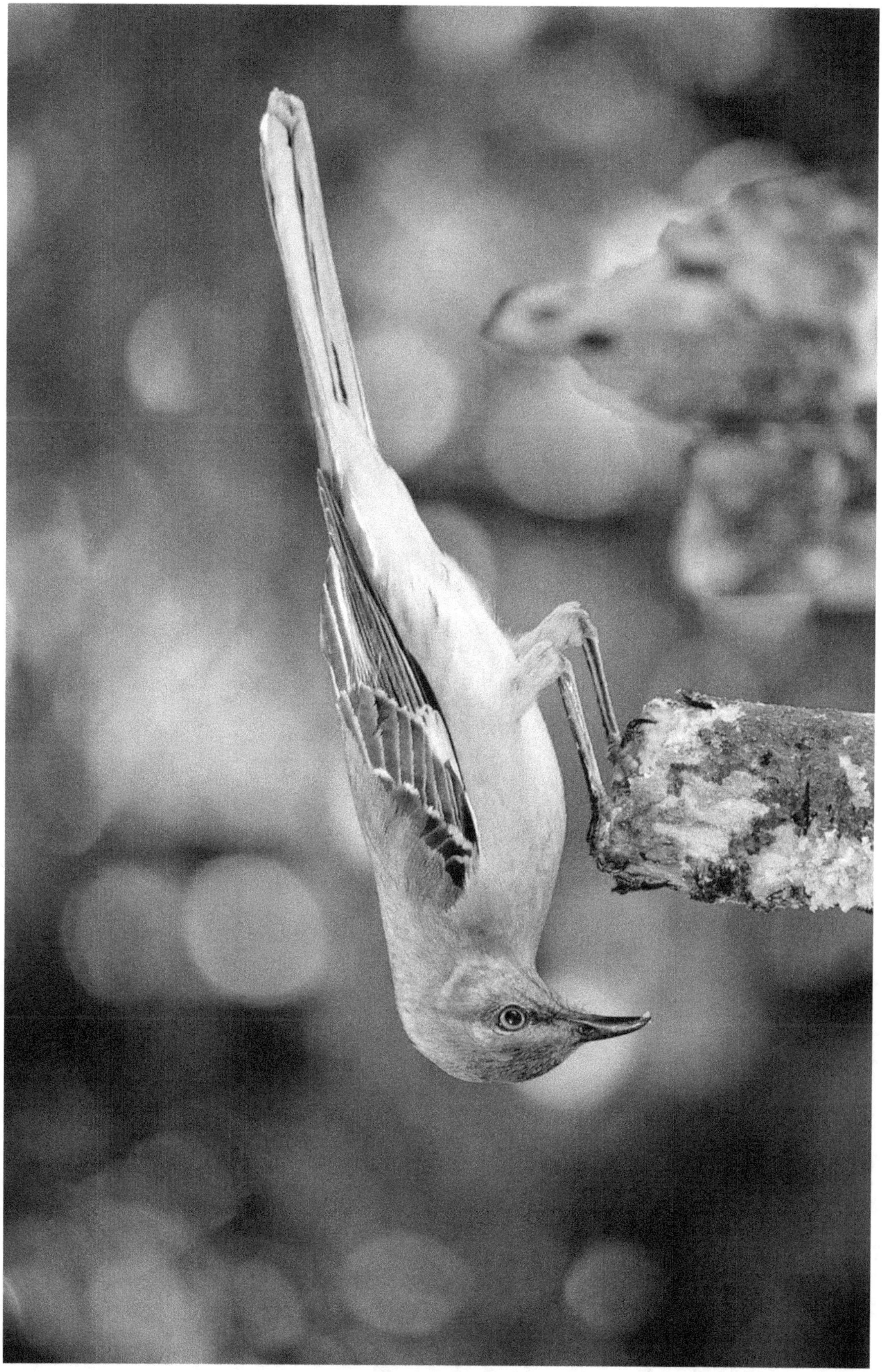

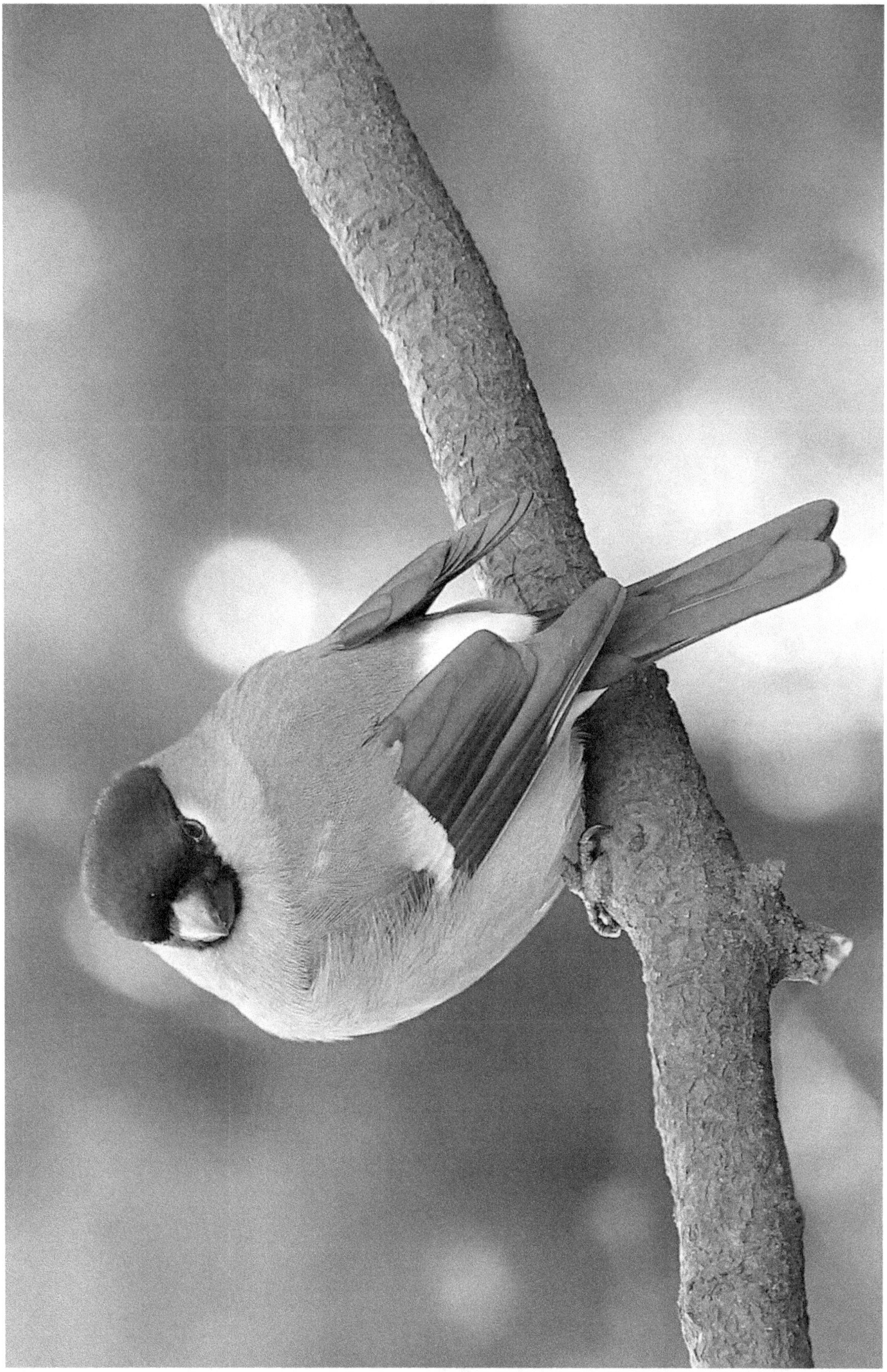

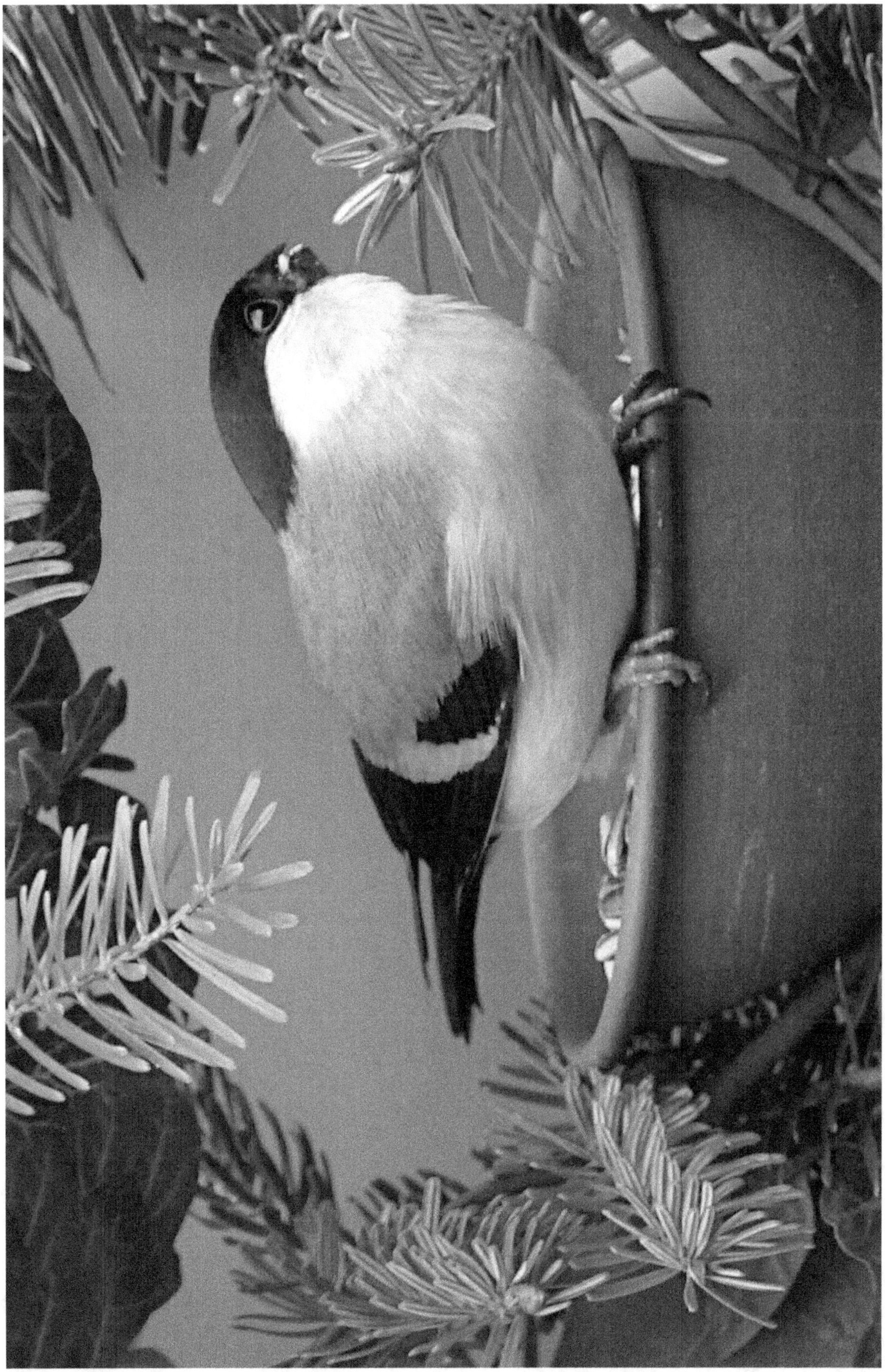

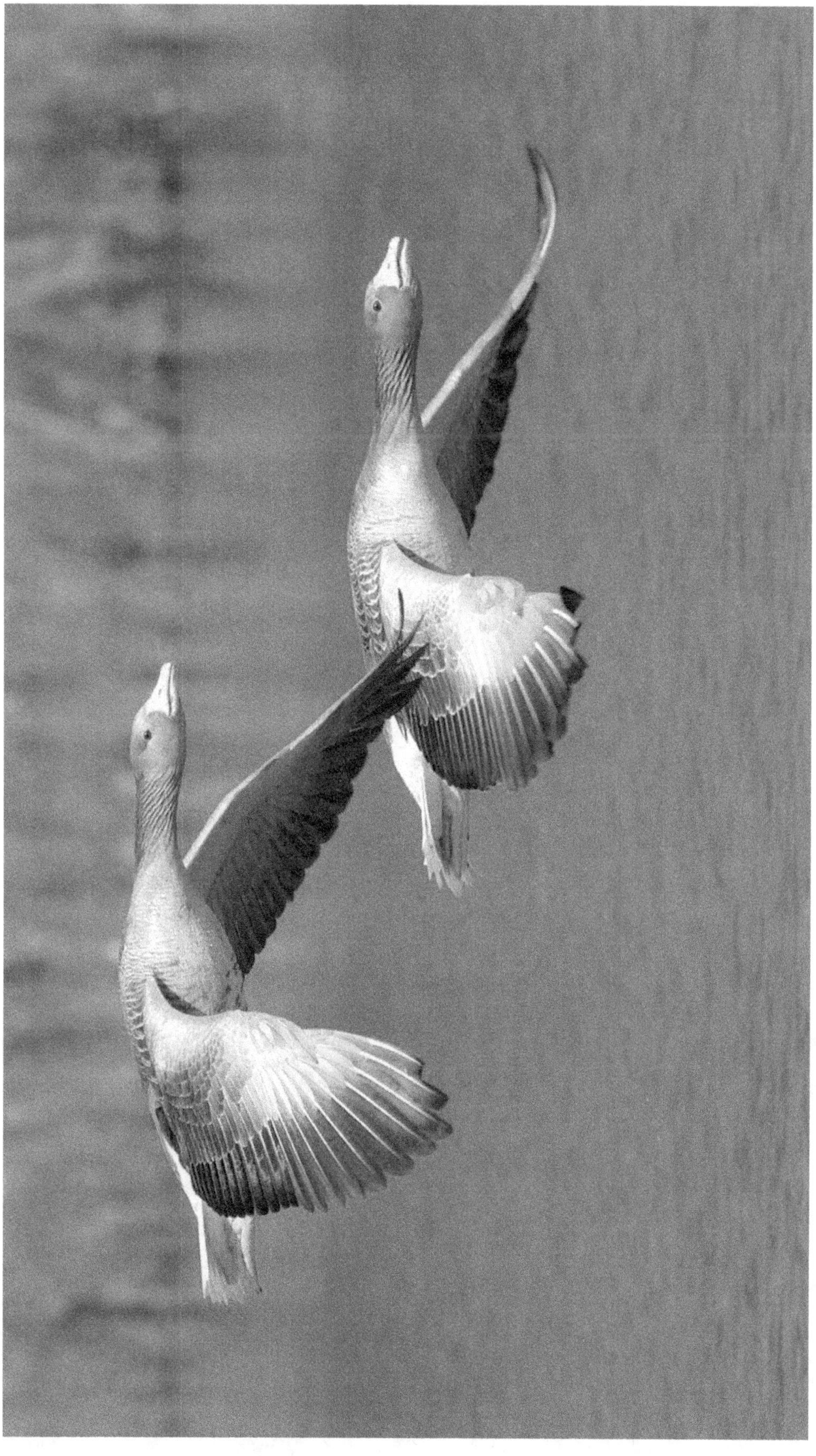

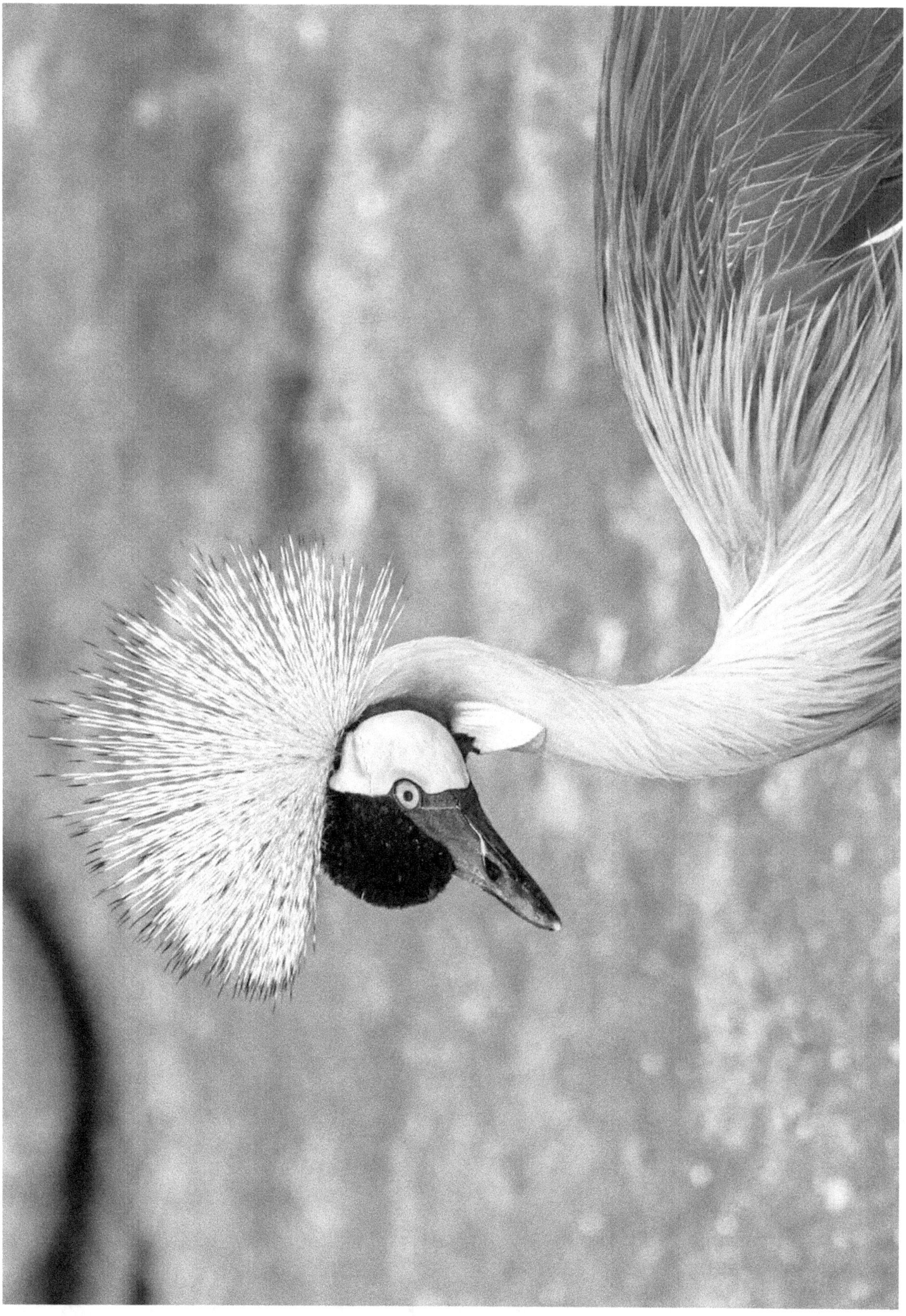

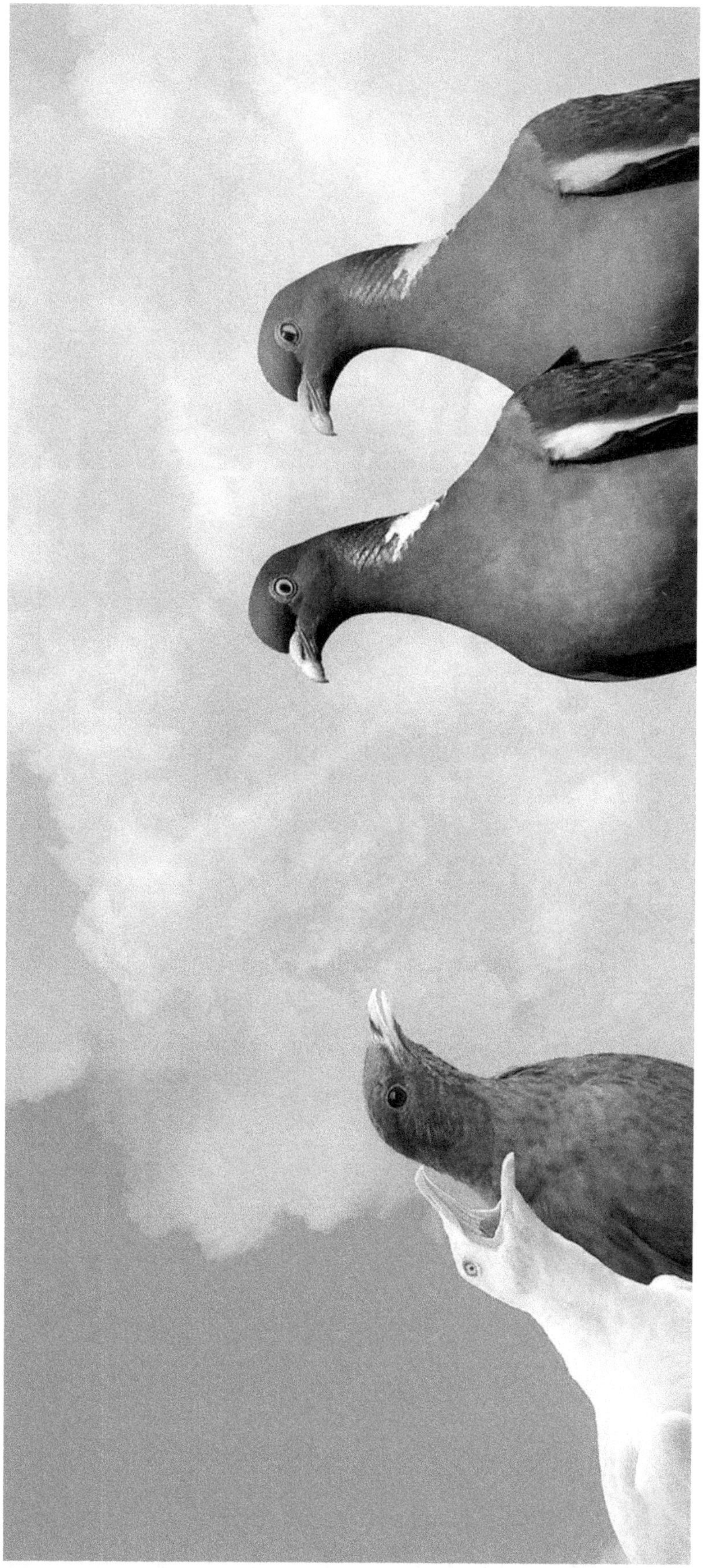

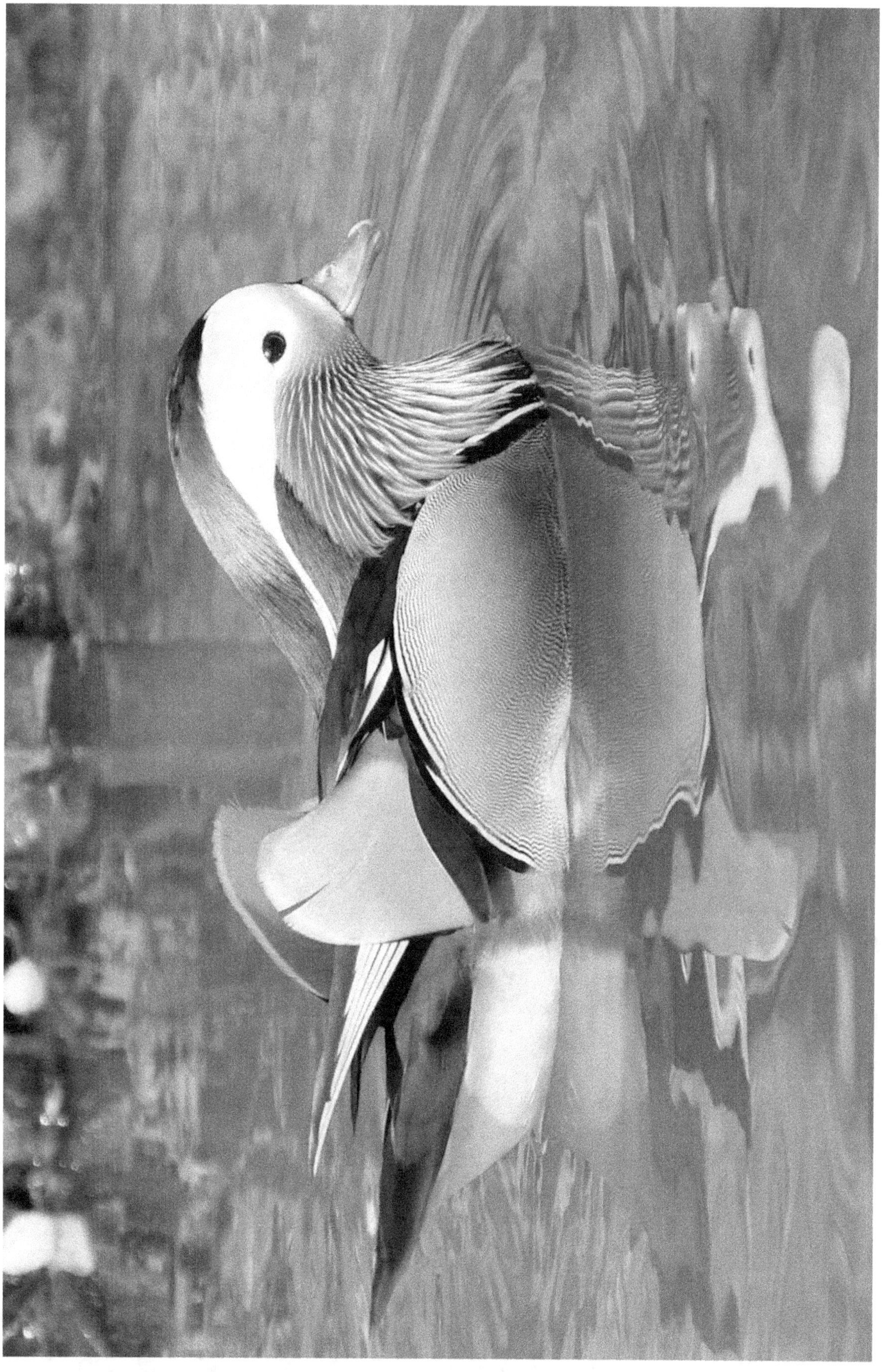

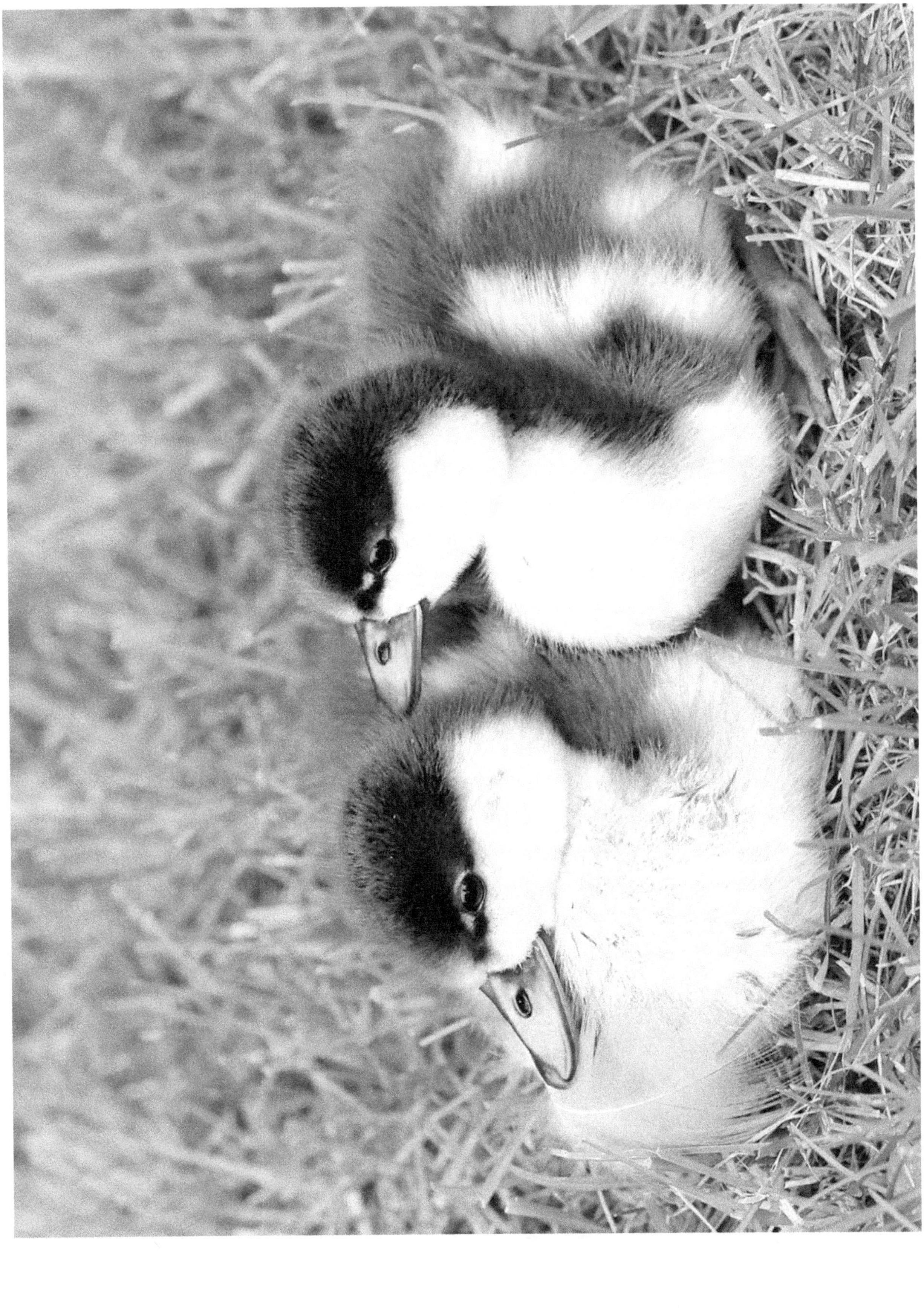

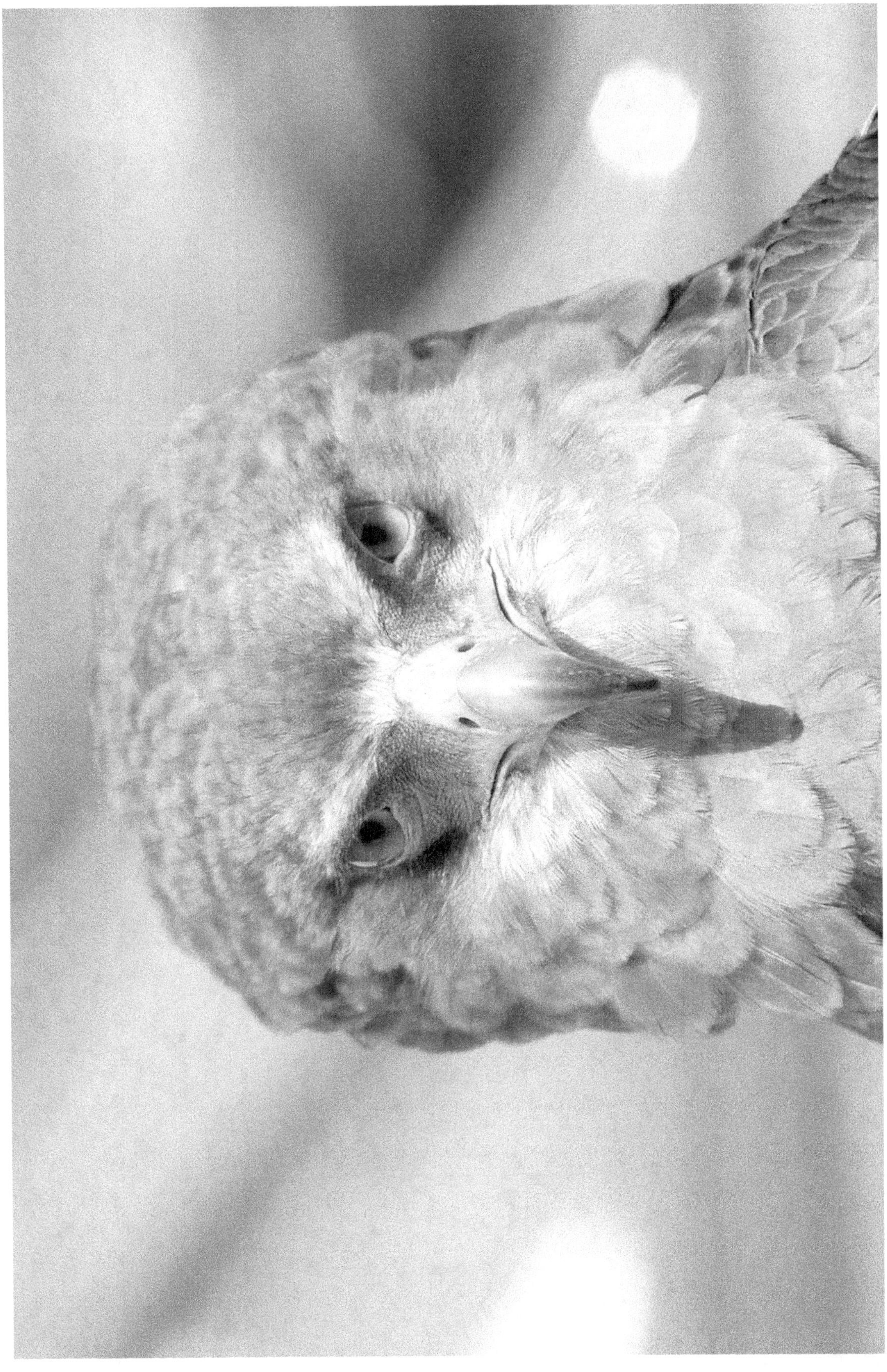

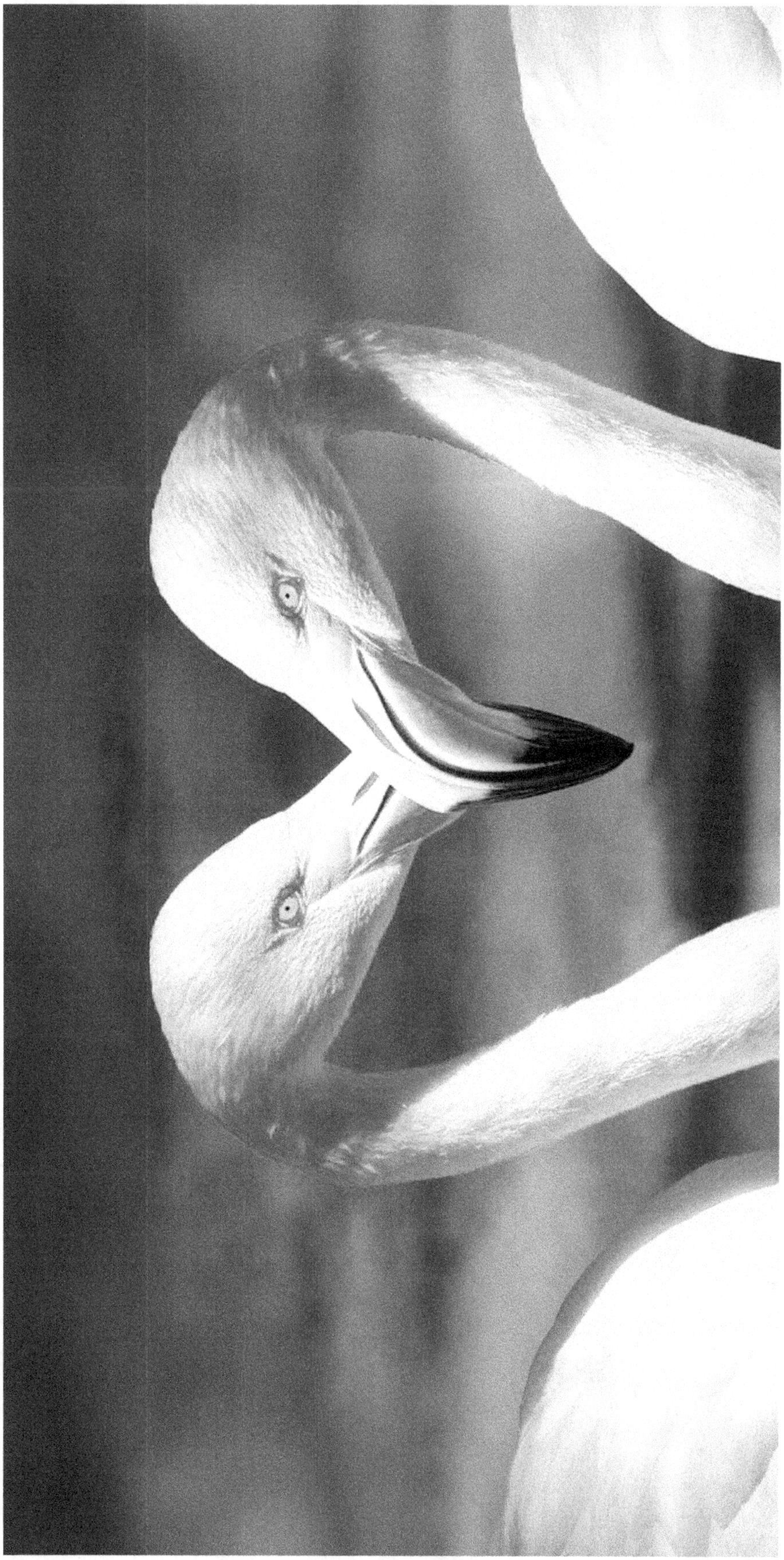

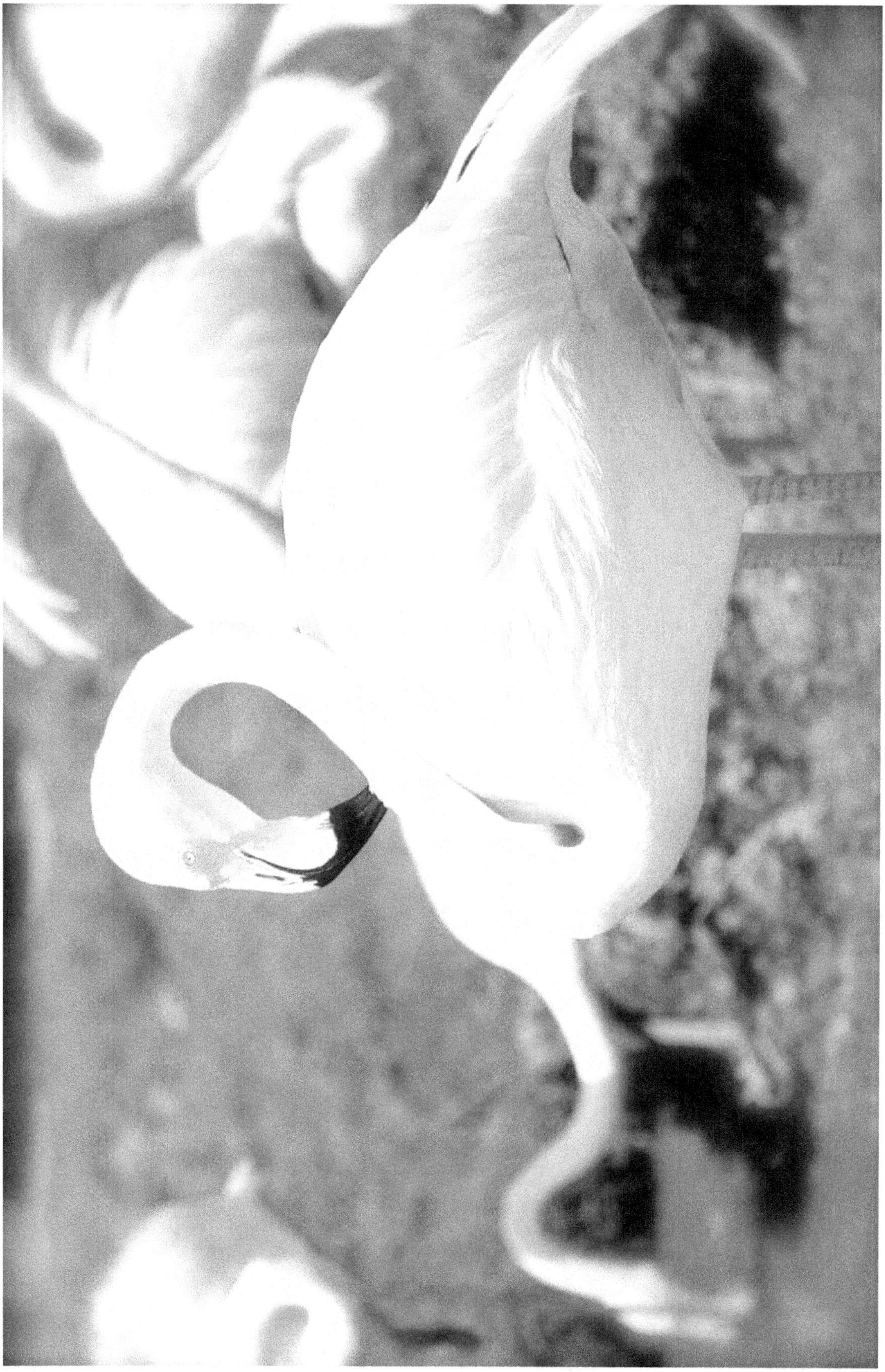

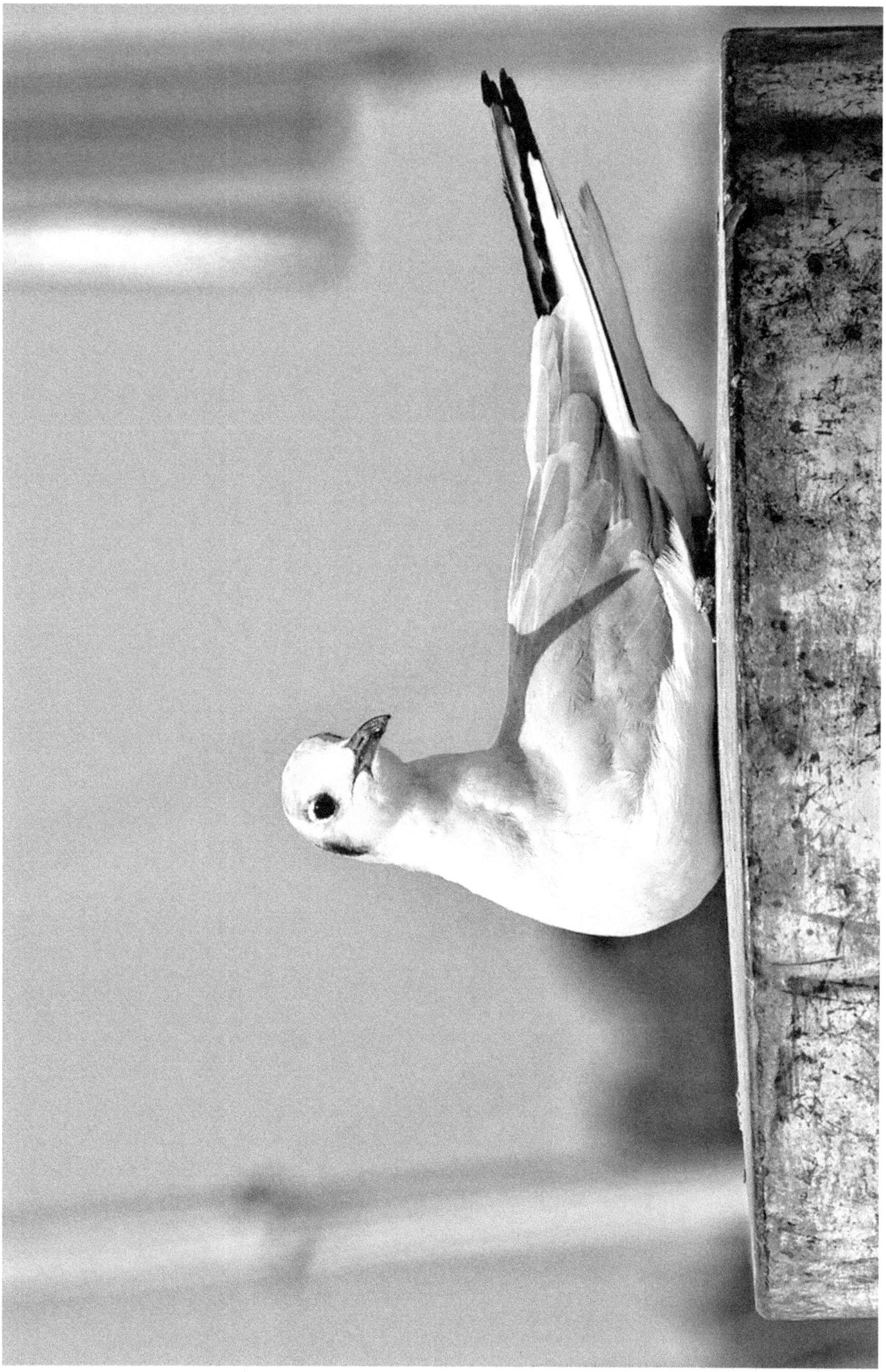

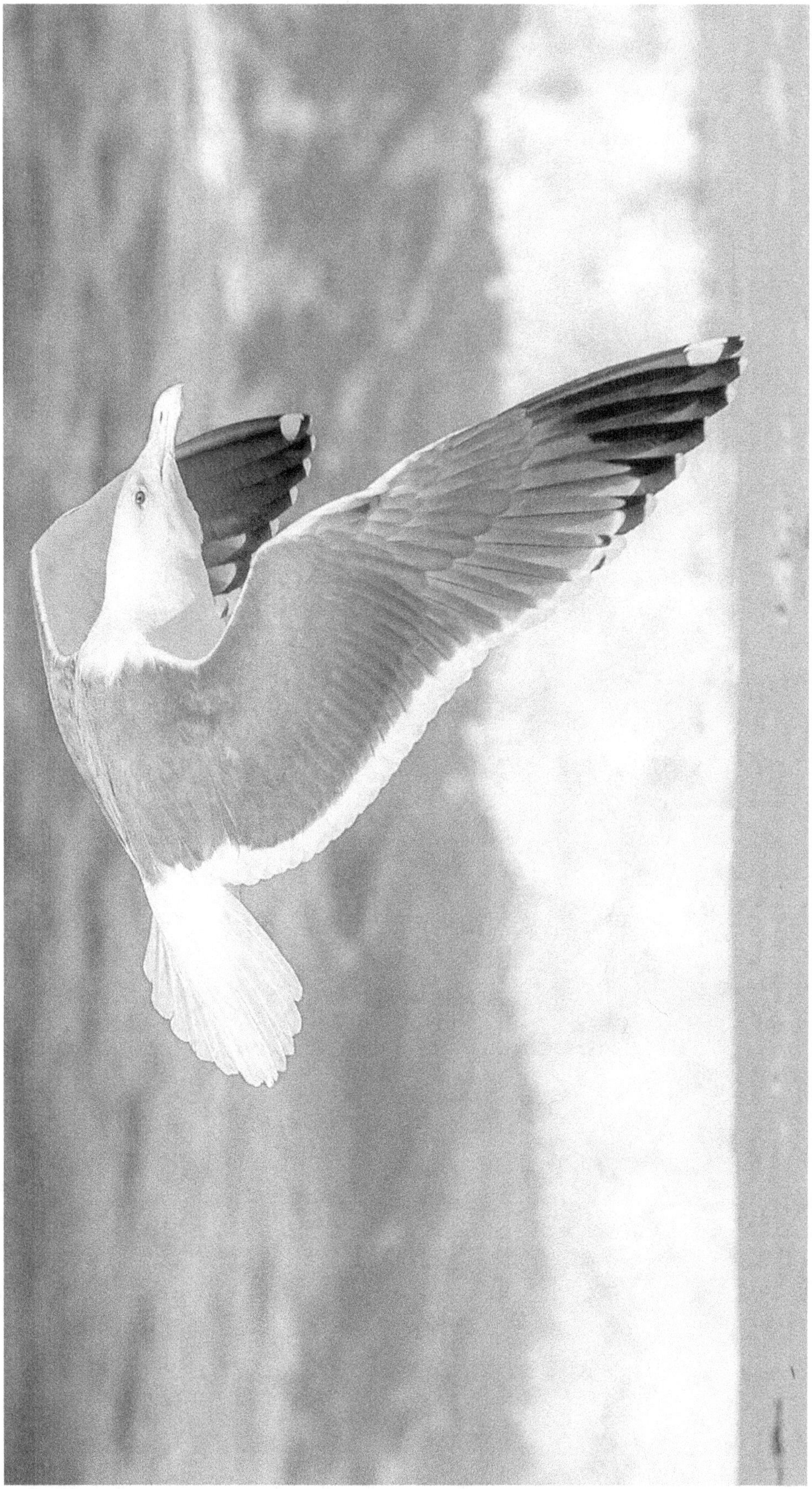

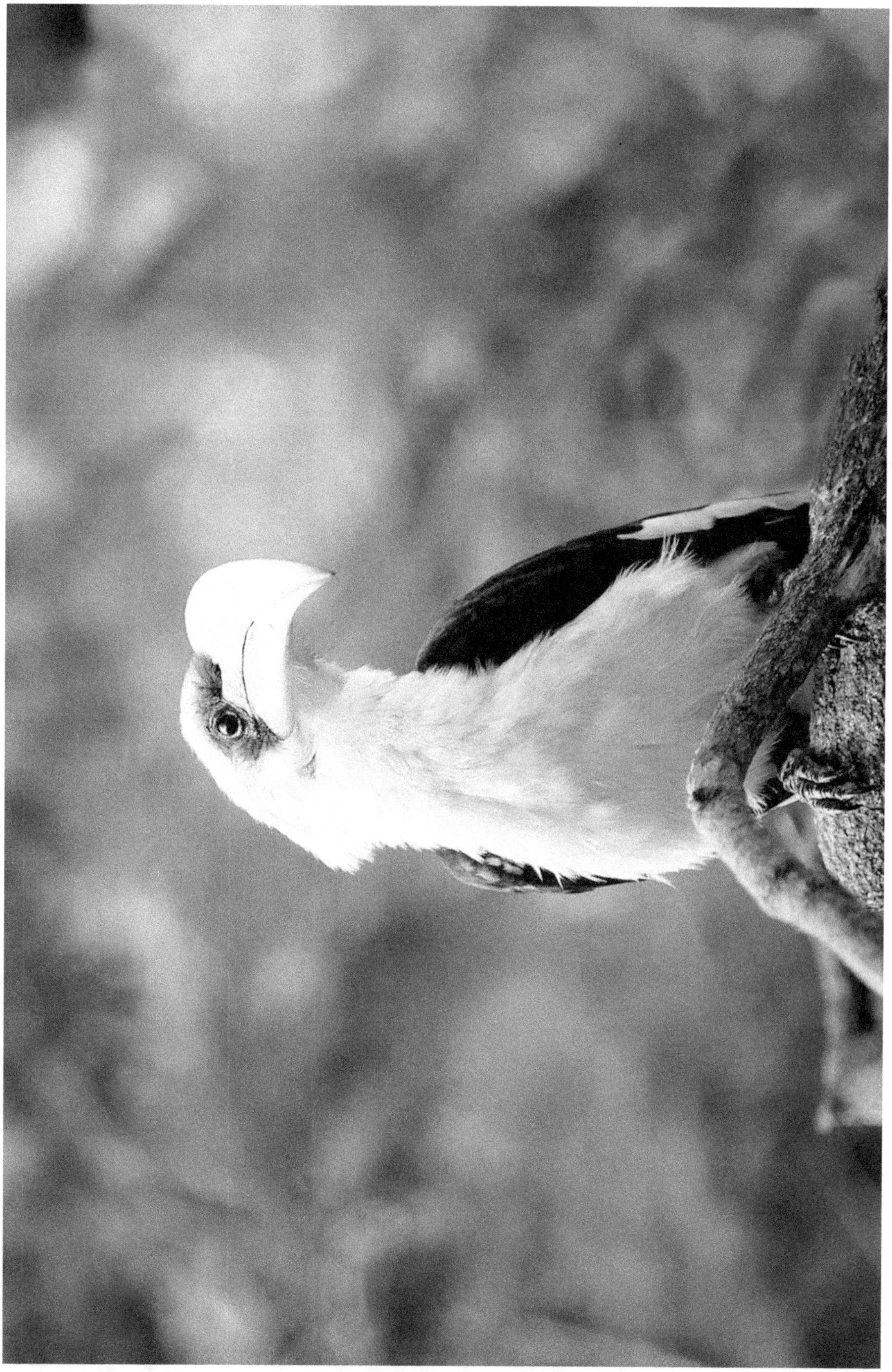

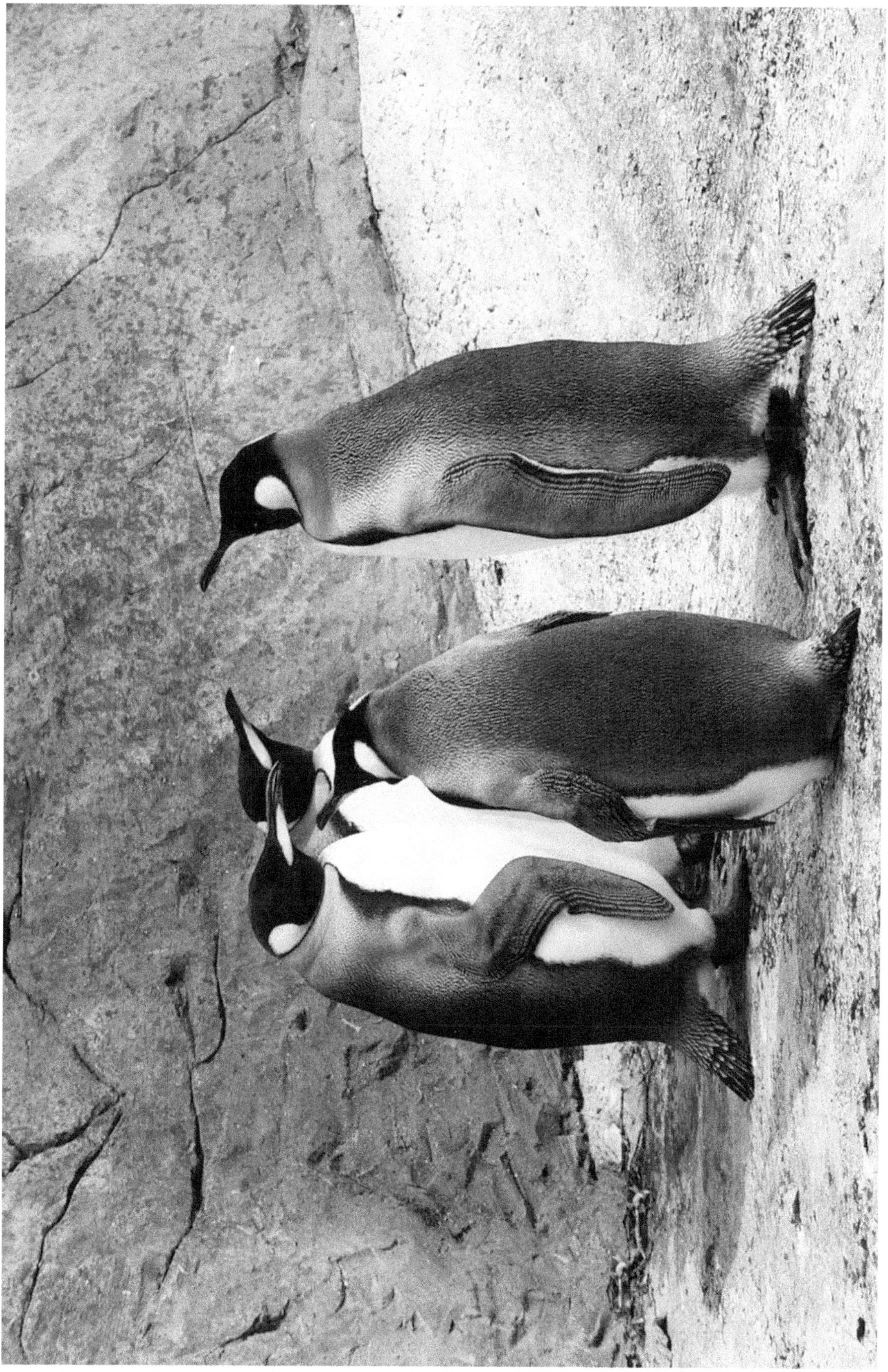

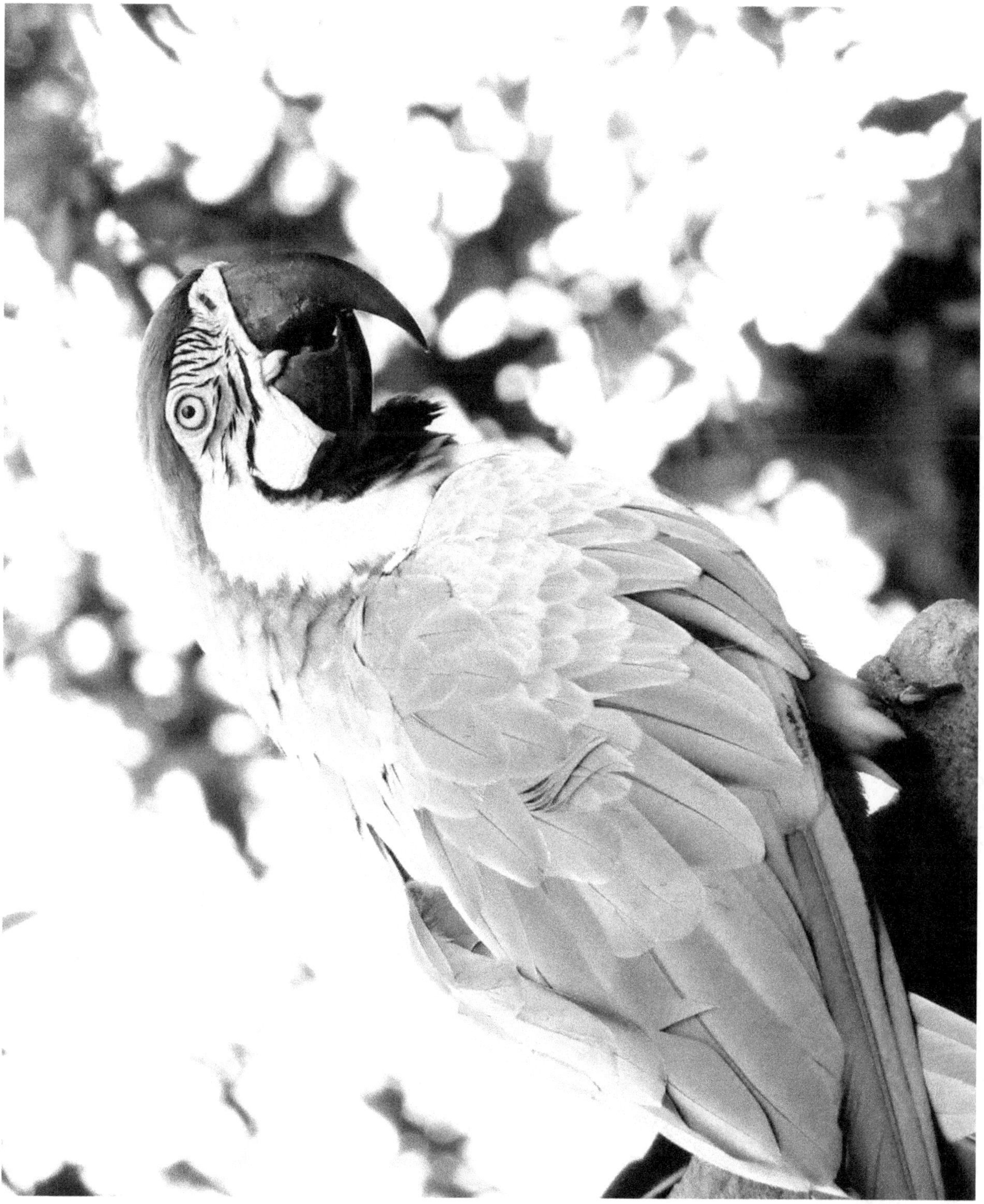

www.ingramcontent.com/pod-product-compliance
Lightning Source LLC
Chambersburg PA
CBHW081119280526
45787CB00007B/2904
9781535157162